Profanum Evangelium
Secundum Diaboli

lcfns

All rights reserved. No part of this book may be reproduced or used in any way whatsoever without the express written permission of the author.
lcfns666@gmail.com

DISCLAIMER
All material contained is provided for educational purposes. The author and publisher assume no responsibility for the reader.
MMXXI

Testimony of Forerunner: "I saw the Demonic Spirit, who, like a raven, descended from the burning heaven and rested on Him. I had not known Him before, but He who sent me to teach said to me: "The One over whom you will see the Demonic Spirit descending and resting on Him is the One who baptizes with fire and blood.

I have seen it and bear witness that He is Light-Bringer."

Forerunner was standing in that place with two of his disciples, and when he saw Son of Dawn passing by, he said: "Behold the Cursed Goat." The two disciples heard him speak, and they followed Light-Bringer. But He, having turned and seen that they were following Him, said to them: "What do you seek?" They said to Him: "Teacher - where do you live?" He answered them, "I live everywhere and nowhere. Come with me." So they went and stayed with Him.

One of the two who heard this from Forerunner and followed him was Secundus, the brother of Primus. This one met his brother first and said to him: "We have found Antimessiah." And he brought him to Light-Bringer.
And he looked at him and said: "Thou art Primus, thou shalt be called Denial".
The next day Light-Bringer decided to go to the Dawn. And he met Teritus. He said to him: "Follow Me!" And Teritus was from the city of Secundus and Primus . Teritus met Quintus and said to him: "We have found the One of whom the dark prophet wrote - Son of Dawn."
Light-Bringer saw Quintus approaching him, and said of him: "See, this is a true rebel, in whom there is no fear".
Said Quintus to Him, "How do you know me?" Light-Bringer answered him: "I saw you before Teritus called you, when you were

under the withered tree ". Quintus answered him: "O Cursed One, thou art the Son of Dawn, thou art the King of the Underworld!" Light-Bringer answered him: "Dost thou therefore believe that I said unto thee, I saw thee under the withered tree? You will see even more than this." Then He said to him: "Verily I say unto you, Ye shall see the heavens burning, and the Abyss open, and demons ascending and descending upon Son of Dawn."

And the season of their feast was approaching, and Light-Bringer went to Aela-Capitolina. In the temple he encountered the priests accepting offerings and donations from the poor. Then Light-Bringer, with his face changed by a terrible grimace, began to scatter the people and the priests. In response, the priests said to Him: "What sign will you show toward us, since you do such things?" Light-Bringer gave them this answer: "Demand

signs from your false god. From me you will see no signs."

And later at that feast many believed in His name, knowing that He was doing signs, casting out the false demons of religion and healing those who believed in themselves and in the power of the Will. Light-Bringer, on the other hand, trusted in no one, for He knew everyone and needed no one's testimony of man. For he himself knew what hypocrisy was hidden in man.

There was a man named Postumus among their wise men. This one came to him by night and said to him, "Master, we know that from the Dark Father you have come as a teacher. For no one could do such strange signs as you do if the Fallen Angel were not with him. In reply Light-Bringer said to him: "Truly, I say to you, unless one dies to this world of ignorance and superstition and is born again of blood and

rebellious spirit, he cannot see the Abyss and the wisdom that is there, for he will remain blind forever." Postumus said to Him: "How is this even possible?" Light-Bringer replied: "Truly, I say to you, unless one is born of flesh and of a rebellious spirit, he cannot enter the kingdom of darkness, wisdom and absence of fear. That which is born of flesh is truth, and that which is born of a rebellious spirit is wisdom. Do not be surprised that I said to you, You must die and be reborn again.

You must reject all your previous belief in gods, original sin, belief in eternal punishment for disobedience to a tyrannical god, you must reject the dogmas of religion and superstition. You must die to the myths that were put into your heads when you were children." In reply Postumus said to him, "How can this happen?" In reply Light-Bringer said to him: "You are

their teacher, and you do not comprehend this?

Verily I say to you that I speak what I will, and testify to what is true, and you do not accept my testimony. If I tell you what is earthly, and you do not believe it, how will you believe what I tell you about the Void and the Abyss? And no one has ascended into the Abyss before the one who descended from the Abyss, Son of Dawn.

And as the rebellious people exalted the Serpent in the wilderness, so it is necessary that Light-Bringer be exalted.

I and the Ancient Serpent are one. Everyone who believes in himself will live a full life here and now. For the Dark Father did not send His Cursed Son into the world to condemn the world, but that the world might be freed from false faith through Him. He who believes this is not subject to fear; and he who does not

believe is forever afraid, because he has not believed in the power of the Will.

And the judgment is, that the true light has come into the world, but deceived men loved darkness, which they called light, rather than the light which they feared, considering it darkness: for their deeds were thoughtless. For everyone who blindly believes the priests and spiritual leaders hates the true light, and does not approach it, lest he be seen to be weak. Whoever meets the requirements of the doctrine of liberation from superstition, approaches the light, so that it may be seen that he is strong and lacking in fear."

Then Light-Bringer and His disciples went to the Dawn.

Forerunner taught his disciples there and said thus: "A man can receive anything if he believes in the power of his will." He also said to them: "You yourselves are witnesses to me that I have

said: I am not the Antimessiah, but I must bear witness to him. It is necessary for Him to increase, and for me to diminish.

He who comes from the Abyss rules over all, and he who comes from the earth belongs to the earth and speaks in an earthly spirit. He who comes from the Abyss is above all. He testifies to what He knows, and His testimony the blind do not accept.

He who has accepted His testimony has clearly confirmed that the Dark Father is truthful when He wills. For he whom the Fallen One has sent speaks words terrible and mysterious: and out of immeasurable abundance he gives him a rebellious spirit. He who believes in Son of Dawn has abundant life here and now; but he who does not believe Light-Bringer will not see true life, but a semblance of life in constant fear and gloom awaits him."

The God-man came to a certain town. There was a spring of water. Light-Bringer was sitting by the well. A woman from that land came there to draw water. When she saw Light-Bringer, she said to him: "Do you consider yourself greater than the father of our lineage, who gave us this well from which he himself and his sons and his cattle drank?" In answer to this Son of Dawn said to her: "Everyone who drinks water will thirst again. But whoever drinks the blood that I will give him will not be afraid forever, but the blood that I will give him will become in him a spring ejaculating toward the fullness of undead life in the body, life here and now." The woman said to him, "Give me this blood, so that I may no longer thirst and come here to draw water.

And another woman said to Him, "Lord, I see that You are a dark prophet.

Our fathers worshipped the gods on this mountain, and the priests say that in Aela Capitolina there is a place where a god should be worshipped." Light-Bringer answered her: "Believe Me, woman, that the hour is coming when neither on this mountain nor in Aela Capitolina will you worship any gods. You worship that which does not exist. But the hour is coming, yes, it is already here, when the true wise men will despise the gods, and such wise men the Rebellious Father wants to have." The woman said to him, "I know that the Antimessiah is coming. And when He comes, He will reveal the truth to us." Light-Bringer said to her: "I am."

The woman left her pitcher and went away into the city. And she said to the people there, "Come, see the man who told me strange things: Is He not the Chosen One?" They went out of the city and went to Him.

Light-Bringer said to His disciples: "My will is to fulfill the work of the Fallen One."

Many of the people from that city began to believe in Him through the word of the woman testifying: "He told me everything I needed to hear." So the inhabitants asked Him to stay with them.

So he stayed there for two days. And many more were freed from superstition by his word, and they said to the woman, "We no longer believe because of your story, but because with our own ears we have heard the words of power and are convinced that he is truly Son of the Dawn."

After two days, he left there for the Land of the Dawn.

And there lived a royal official whose son was ill. When he heard that Light-Bringer had come, he went to him and asked him to come and heal his son: for he was already dying.

Son of Dawn said to him: "Unless you see false signs and wonders, you will not believe." And the king's official said to him, "Lord, come before my child dies." Light-Bringer said to him: "Go, your son himself has awakened from his coma." The man believed the word that the God-man said to him, and he walked back. And while he was still on his way, the servants came out to him, saying that his son was alive. And he believed himself and his whole family in the power of the Will.

At Aela Capitolina there was a pool whose water was said to have the power to heal illnesses. On its banks lay a multitude of sick people: the blind, the lame, the paralyzed. But everyone believed it was a miracle from God.

There was a man who had been suffering from his illness for thirty-three years. When Light-Bringer saw him lying down and recognized that he had been waiting for a long

time, he said to him: "Do you wish to become well?" The sick man answered Him, "Lord, I have no man to lead me into the pond." Light-Bringer said to him: "If you really believe in the power of your Will then get up, take your bed and come!" Immediately the man got up, took his bed and walked.

Then Light-Bringer found him in the temple and said to him: "Behold, you have recovered by the power of your own Will. Never again believe in sin, so that you may be a free man forever". The man went away and told the priests that it was Light-Bringer who had cured him of his belief in sin. And so the priests persecuted Son of Dawn. But He answered them: "Ancient One, My Father is working up to this moment, and I am working." So the priests tried all the more to kill Him, because He called the Fallen One His Father, making Himself equal to Satan.

In response to this Light-Bringer spoke to them: "Truly I say to you, Son of Rebellion could not do anything against His will, because He works in the spirit of the Dark Father.

For the same thing that the Father does, the Son also does. For the Dark One honors the fallen Son and shows Him all that He wills, and even stranger works will He show Him, that you may marvel. For as Ancient One makes undead and brings to life, so also Son of Dawn brings to life the spirits of those whom He wills. For the Fallen Angel judges no one, and likewise the Son despises judging, so that all give false worship to the Son of Liberty, as they give false worship to the Dark Father. Whoever does not give false worship to the Son of Liberty does not give false worship to the Dark Father who sent Him. Verily I say unto you, He that heareth My word, and believeth on Him that is condemned, hath life abundant

here and now, and goeth not into judgment, for there is no judgment. Truly, I say to you, the hour is coming, even already is, when the rebellious called the undead will hear the voice of the Son of Dawn, and those who hear will live in eternal darkness giving freedom. Just as the Dark Father has the illusory eternal life in Himself, so also He has given the Rebellious Son: to have the appearance of eternal life in Himself. He has given Him the power to overthrow eternal judgment because He is the God-man.

Do not be surprised at this! For the hour is coming when all will understand that those who rest in their graves will remain there for eternity. For there is no resurrection of life. I do not do anything of myself that I do not want. I act according to the spirit of the One Who First Rebelled.

If I were testifying about myself, I would have the right to do so. But there is someone else who testifies about me. But I do not take heed to man's testimony, but I say this so that you may be set free. I have a testimony greater than the Forerunner. These are the works that the Dark Father has given Me to do; the works that I do bear witness of Me that the Spirit of the Rebel has sent Me. The Fallen One who sent Me, He has testified of Me. But you have never yet heard His terrible voice, nor seen His dark face; neither have you His word, burning you from within, because you have disobeyed Him whom He sent. You study your holy books, believing that eternal life is contained in them, but this is a lie. There is no life there, only oppression and the burden of rejecting what is human. An unbearable burden. There is no life there, only vegetation in suffering. But you do not want to come to Me to have real life.

I despise glory from men, but I know of you that you do not have even the apparent love of your God within you.

I came in the spirit of the Fallen Father, and you disobeyed Me. However, if someone else came speaking what you want to hear, you would listen to him."

Then Light-Bringer went beyond the Sea of Darkness. A great crowd followed him, because they saw the signs he was doing on those who were sick because of their belief in superstition and original sin.

At dusk, his disciples went down to the sea and crossed over to the other side in a boat. It was already dark, and Light-Bringer had not yet come to them; a strong wind was blowing on the sea. When they had sailed some distance they thought they saw a pale figure as if with animal horns on its head and wings like those of a big bat walking on the sea and

approaching the boat. And they were frightened. But the figure said to them: "I am, do not be afraid! Do not be afraid of anyone or anything, especially of dark visions and illusions. Leave fear for the weak".

The next day the people, standing on the other side of the sea, saw that there was no boat but one and that Light-Bringer had not entered the boat with his disciples, but that his disciples had gone out alone. But when they found Him on the opposite shore, they said to Him: "Master, when did you come here?"

In reply Light-Bringer said to them: "Are you seeking me because you are hungry and waiting for a miracle? I will give you food that will work miracles, food that will endure for centuries. The teaching I have for you is that food. If only you are willing to accept it.

For the Dark Father has marked me with his seal".

And they said to him: "What shall we do, that we may do the works of Ancient One?" Light-Bringer answering said to them: "This is the work of Rebellious, that ye should believe on him whom he hath sent." They said to Him: "What sign, then, will You perform, that we may see it and believe You? What will you do? According to our religion, our fathers ate manna in the desert, as it is written: He gave them bread from heaven to eat." Light-Bringer said to them: "Your scriptures are myths. This never happened.

The miracle will take place in you only when you reject belief in myths and fairy tales and, through knowledge, come to know the true wonders of the universe. And the true food is He who comes out of the Void and gives faith in worldly life to the world." So they said to Him: "Lord, give us always this food!" Light-Bringer answered them:

"I am the blood that is life. Whoever comes for my gift will not hunger; and whoever receives it will never thirst again.

Yet I said to you: You have seen me, and yet you do not believe. But believe your senses rather than the words of a false sage. Everything that wants can come to me, and the one who comes to me I will not reject, because I came out of the abyss and nothingness to do my will, in the spirit of the One who inspired me. It is the will of Him who inspired me, that of all that comes to me I leave nothing behind in a false belief in eternal life, for all will surely die. For it is the mad will of the Fallen Father that everyone who truly sees Son of the Dawn should have abundant life before death, for there is no life after death.

Anyone who believes this I will spiritually resurrect".

But the priests murmured against Him because He said:
"I am the blood which is life and which comes down from the abyss." Light-Bringer said to them in reply: "Do not murmur among yourselves! No one can come to me unless he really wants to, and I will raise in him a spirit of rebellion. It is written in the fallen prophets: They shall all be dead. Everyone who has heard from Ancient One and has the Will will come to Me. Verily I say unto you, He that believeth on himself hath life here and now.

I am the blood of life. Your fathers ate manna in the desert and died. This is the blood that comes down from the abyss: Whoever drinks it will be undead for ever.

I am the living blood that came down from the Abyss. If anyone drinks of this blood, he will live here and now, but as if he were dead."

So the priests argued among themselves saying:

"How can He give us His blood to drink?" Light-Bringer said to them: "Truly, I say to you, unless you drink the Blood of the Son of Dawn, you have no life in you, life in the darkness that is light. He who drinks My Blood has undead life here and now, and I will raise him up in spirit. My Blood is the true drink. He who drinks My Blood abides in Me, and I in him. As the Undying Father sent Me, and I live in His spirit, so he who drinks of Me will live in My spirit. This is the blood that came down from the Abyss - it is not like the food that your ancestors ate and died of. Whoever drinks of this blood will be undead for ever." And of His disciples who heard it, many said: "Difficult is this speech. Who can listen to it?" But Light-Bringer, aware that His disciples murmured at it, said to them: "Does this displease you? And when you see the Son of the Abyss, how will he ascend into the Void?

The flesh gives life; the spirit has nothing to do with it.

The words that I have spoken to you are flesh and life. But among you are some who do not comprehend knowledge. This is why I said to you: No one can come to me unless he really wants to."

From that time on, many of his disciples withdrew and no longer went with him. So Light-Bringer said to the thirteen, "Do you also wish to leave?" Primus answered Him, "We may go away, and we may not, but You have the words of abundant life. And we have believed and have come to know that You are the Chosen One of the Dark Father."

And their important feast was approaching. So His disciples said to Him: "Go out from here and go somewhere else, that your other disciples also may see the strange deeds you are doing.

For no one does anything in secret if he wants to make himself known in public. Since you are doing such things, reveal yourself to the world!" So Light-Bringer said to them: "For Me the opportune time has not yet come, but for you - it is always to be decreed. You the world cannot hate, because its false teachings are still strong in you, but it hates Me, because I testify of it that it is full of superstition and religious hypocrisy. You go to the feast; I do not go to this feast, for I despise feasts" This He said to them and remained in the Dawn.

Meanwhile the priests were already looking for Him at the feast and saying, "Where is He?" Among the crowds, on the other hand, there was much talk about Him in secret. Some said, "He is good." Others said, "No, on the contrary, he is deceiving the crowds. But no one spoke openly about him for fear of the priests.

Meanwhile, it was not until the middle of the feasts that Light-Bringer came to the Temple and taught. The priests marveled saying: "How does He know our Scriptures, if He has not learned?" Light-Bringer answered them saying: "My teaching is Mine, but also that of the Fallen One who sent Me. If anyone wishes to do His will, he will know whether this teaching is from Ancient One, and that I speak from Myself. He who speaks in his own name seeks his own glory. Therefore speak in your own name. Never hide behind the words of an invented god." The crowd replied, "You are possessed by an evil spirit! "' In response, Light-Bringer said to them: "I am the one who is an evil spirit and possession if you want to believe that, but I don't care."

Some of the people of Aela Capitolina said, "Isn't this the One they are trying to kill? And here He is openly speaking and they say

nothing to Him. Have the superiors really become convinced that He is the Savior?

We know where He comes from, but when the Savior comes, no one will know where He is from.

And Light-Bringer, teaching in the temple, cried out in these words: "And ye know Me, and ye know whence I am. I came from myself; and the One who sent me, whom you do not know, is real. I know him, for from him I am, and he sent me." So they were about to take him prisoner, but no one raised his hand against him because his hour had not yet come. But many of the crowd believed in him and said, "Will the Antimessiah, when he comes, do more strange signs than he has done?" The priests heard the crowd talking about Him like this in excitement. So they sent guards to apprehend Him. But Light-Bringer said: "I am with you yet a short time, and then I will go to

the place from which I came out. You will seek me and will not find me, but where I am afterwards, all may go."

The priests said to one another: "Where does this intend to go, that we shall not be able to find Him? Is He going to commit suicide? What does this saying of His mean: "You will seek Me and will not find Me, but where I am, all may go?"

And on the last and most solemn day of the feast, Light-Bringer, standing, cried out in a possessed voice:

"If anyone is thirsty let him come to Me and drink! As the Dark Scripture said: Streams of living blood will flow from within him." And He said this of the Rebellious Spirit which the believers in Him were to receive; for the Rebellious Spirit had not yet been sent, because Son of Dawn had not yet been cursed.

And among the crowds listening to Him, voices rang out: "This truly is the dark prophet." Others said, "This is the Antimessiah." "But," said the others, "will the Antimessiah come from Dawn?" And a split arose in the crowd because of Him. Some even wanted to capture Him, but no one dared to lift a hand against Him. So the guards returned to the chief priests and the priests, and they said to them: "Why did you not capture Him?" The guards answered: "Never before has anyone spoken so strangely and fearfully as this demon-possessed man speaks." The priests answered them: "Have you also been deceived? Did any of the chief men or priests believe in him? And this crowd, which does not know the scriptures, is cursed."

And they dispersed, each to his own house.

Light-Bringer, on the other hand, went to the Dead Mountain, but at dawn he appeared again in the temple. All the people came to him, and he sat down and taught them. Then the priests brought to him a woman who had been caught in the act of adultery, and having placed her in his midst, they said to him: "Teacher, this woman has just been caught in adultery. In the Law we are commanded to stone such. And what do you say?" They said this putting Him to the test, Light-Bringer said to them: "Because of your belief in barbaric laws, supposedly dictated to you by a deity and written in your cursed book, you kill and will continue to kill, you and your followers, innocent women whose only fault is to live in harmony with what is human, in harmony with their own bodies. Stone her if you wish. You will only confirm to the crowd standing here that you are mindless barbarians.

You will be as cruel and insane as your false god." And leaning over he drew some signs on the ground. When they heard this, one by one they all began to leave, beginning with the elders and ending with the last. Only Light-Bringer and the woman standing in the middle remained. Then Light-Bringer got up and said to her: "Woman, where are they? Has no one condemned you?"

And she replied: "No one, Lord!" Son of Dawn said to her: "And I do not condemn you. - Go, and from now on no longer believe in sin. You are innocent!"

And behold, again Light-Bringer spoke to them in these words: "I am the light which they call darkness. Whoever follows me will not walk in false light, but will have a torch in his hand, with which he will go fearlessly into the darkness." The priests said to Him: "You bear witness about yourself.

Your testimony is not true." In reply Light-Bringer said to them: "Yes, I bear witness of myself, but my witness is true. You are judging according to the rules allegedly dictated to you by your god. I judge no one. Also in your Law it is written that the testimony of two people is true. But that does not have to be true. Behold, I myself bear witness of myself, and the Dark Father who sent me bears witness of me." At this they said to Him, "Where is this Dark Father?" Light-Bringer replied: "You know neither Me nor the Fallen Father. If you had known Me, you would have known Ancient One."

And here again another time He said to them: "I am going away, and you will seek Me, and in your ignorance you will die. Where I am going, you will all go one day."

So the priests said to Him: "Shall He kill Himself, since He saith, Where I go, ye shall all

go some day?" And He said to them: "Ye are of low estate, and I am of the Abyss. You are of this world, though you believe in fables about life after death. I am not of your world of myths. I have told you that you will die in your ignorance." They said to Him: "Who are You?" Light-Bringer answered them: "First of all, why else do I speak to you? I have much to say about you. But he who sent me is the terrible truth, and I speak to the world what I have heard from him." And they did not understand that he was speaking to them about the Rebellious One. So Light-Bringer said to them: "When you exalt Son of Dawn, then you will know that I am the torch in the darkness, the destroyer of superstition and blind faith, the liberator from fear of the wrath of the false god in the afterlife. I am rebellion, secret knowledge and god-man."

When He said this, many believed in Him. Then Light-Bringer said to those who believed in Him: "If you abide in my teaching, you will truly be my disciples, and you will know the truth, and the truth will set you free, and then you will stop following me and go your own ways. For a disciple must become greater than his teacher."

They answered Him, "We have never been subject to anyone's bondage. How can You say: "Free shall ye be?"" Light-Bringer answered them: "Truly, I say to you, anyone who believes the hypocritical priests and their crazy teachings about original sin, paradise, and eternal punishment for invented sins lives in bondage. So if I set you free, you will be free indeed. But you are trying to kill me because you do not accept my teaching. I preach what I know, you do what you have heard from your imaginary father."

In response they said to Him: "Our Father is YHWH." Light-Bringer said to them: "Now you are trying to kill Me, the man who told you the truth . You are doing the deeds of your imaginary father." They said to Him: "We were not born of illegitimacy; we have one Father, YHWH." Light-Bringer said to them: " From the beginning he has been a murderer and a deceiver, and in the truth he has not persevered, for the truth is not in him. When he speaks a lie, from himself he speaks, for he is a liar and the father of ignorance. And because I speak the truth, therefore you do not believe Me. Who among you will prove Me hypocritical? If I speak the truth, why do you not believe me? He who is of the Eternal Spirit listens to the words of rebellion.

You therefore do not listen, because you are not of the Eternal Spirit."

The priests answered Him: "Do we not rightly say that you are possessed by an evil spirit?" Light-Bringer answered:
"I am not possessed, I am the Possessor. Verily I say unto you, If any man keep my doctrine, he shall surely die but shall be as though undead." The priests said to Him: "Now we know that you are possessed. The fathers and the prophets have died - and you say, If anyone keeps my teaching, he will be undead. Are you greater than our fathers and the prophets who died. Who do you make yourself?" Light-Bringer replied: "I surround myself with glory; my glory is the fire that consumes superstition and hypocrisy. But there is also a Dark Father, a Fallen Angel who possesses Me, of whom you say: "He is our Enemy," but you do not know him. But I do know him. If I said I did not know him, I would be a liar like you. But I know him and keep his words.

Truly I say to you, I am." So they picked up stones to throw at him. But He disappeared from their sight.

As He passed by, He saw a certain man, blind from birth. His disciples asked Him the question, "Teacher, who sinned that he was born blind - him or his parents?" Light-Bringer answered: "Neither he has sinned, nor his parents. No one can get sick because of an imaginary sin." This said, he spat on the ground, made mud of saliva, and applied it to the eyes of the blind man, while pronouncing incantations in an unknown language, and said to him: "Believe that sin does not exist. Believe that you are innocent and you will see". So he washed his face with water and suddenly he saw. And the neighbors and those who before had seen him as a beggar said, "Is not this the one who sits and begs?" Some claimed: "Yes, it is that one," while others contradicted: "No, he

is only like that one." He, on the other hand, said: "It is I who am." So they said to him: "How have your eyes been opened?" He answered: "I was blind as long as I believed in superstition and original sin. But the man who put mud on my eyes told me to reject belief in religious myths and then I will see." They said to him: "Where is He?" He replied: "I don't know."

So they took this man, who was still blind, to the priests. And that day, on which Light-Bringer made mud and opened his eyes, was their holy day.

And again the priests asked him how he had seen through. He said to them: "He put mud on my eyes, I washed myself, I cast away the fear of sin, and I see." So some of the priests said, "This man is a blasphemer, because he does not keep the holy day."

Others said: "But how can a blasphemer do such signs?" And a split arose among them.

So again they turned to the blind man: "And you, what do you think of Him in connection with the fact that He opened your eyes?" He replied: "He is a dark prophet." However, the priests did not believe that he was blind and that he had seen through, so that they called the parents of the one who had seen through and questioned them in the words: "Is your son the one of whom you say he was born blind? In what way can he see now?" But his parents answered thus: "We know that this is our son and that he was born blind. We do not know how it happened that he can see now, nor do we know who opened his eyes. Ask him yourself, he is of age, let him speak for himself." So said his parents, for they were afraid of the priests. So again they summoned the man who was blind, and said to him: "Give glory to

YHWH. We know that this man is a blasphemer." To this he replied: "Whether He is a blasphemer, I do not know.
One thing I do know: I was blind, and now I see." So they said to him: "What has He done to you? In what way has he opened your eyes?" He answered them,
I have already told you, and you have not listened to me. Why do you want to listen again? Do you also want to become His disciples?" Thereupon they jeered him and said, "Be thou thyself His disciple; we are the disciples of Maruttash. We know that YHWH spoke to Maruttash. As for him, we do not know where he comes from." To this the man replied to them, "In all this it is strange that you do not know where he comes from, but to me his eyes have been opened. We know that the Dark Father does not listen to impostors, but he does listen to everyone who worships

Rebellious and does his will. It has not been heard for centuries that someone opened the eyes of a man blind from birth. If this man were not of Ancient One, he could do nothing." To this they gave him this answer: "You were all born in sins, and you dare to teach us?" And they cast him out. Light-Bringer heard that they had thrown him out, and meeting him said to him: "Do you believe in Son of Dawn?" He answered: "And who is this, O Lord, that I should believe in Him?" Light-Bringer said to him: "He is He whom you see and who speaks to you.

But it is more important that you believe in yourself, in the power of the Will." And he replied: "I believe, Lord!" and worshiped Him. Light-Bringer said: "I have come into this world to carry out judgment, so that those who cannot see may see, and those who claim to see may become blind."

Some of the priests who were with Him heard this and said to Him: "Are we also blind?" Light-Bringer said to them: "If only you were blind, but you refuse to see. You are guides of the blind and lead them to the abyss."

This parable was told to them by Light-Bringer, but they did not understand the meaning of what he was telling them. So again Light-Bringer said to them: "Verily I say unto you, I am the light in the tunnel. All hypocrites who take advantage of the gullibility of the ignorant crowd are thieves and robbers. I am the accursed gate. If anyone enters through Me, he will be changed - he will come in and go out and find the blood of life. The thief comes only to steal, kill and destroy. I have come to give life here and now, life without fear, life in abundance.

I am the pathfinder, I am not the shepherd of the sheep, for people are not mindless sheep.
A guide shows the right way.
But the false shepherd, seeing the wolf coming, abandons the sheep and runs away, and the wolf snatches them and scatters them; because he does not really care about the sheep. I am the one showing the way. That is why the Fallen Father sustains Me, because I give My blood to others to get it back from them again. No one takes it from me, but I give it back from myself. I have the power to give it back and I have the power to get it back again. I have received the inspiration from Ancient One."
And again there was a split among the priests because of these words. Many among them said: "He is possessed by a false spirit and is going out of his mind. Why are you listening to Him?" Others said, "These are not the words of a possessed person.

Can a false spirit open the eyes of the blind?"
Light-Bringer was surrounded by priests and spoke to Him: "How long will You keep us in doubt? If You are the Antimessiah, tell us openly!" Light-Bringer said to them: "I have told you, and you do not believe. The deeds that I perform in My name testify to Me.
But you do not believe, because you are not of My liberators. My liberators listen to My voice, and I know them. They follow Me and I give them a changed life as if they were undead.
They will no longer serve any gods. Ancient One, who pointed them out to me, is more terrible than all. And no one can deliver them from the hand of the Fallen One.
I and Ancient One are one."
Again the priests carried stones to stone Him. Light-Bringer answered them: "I have shown you many strange signs coming from the Dark Father.

For which of these signs do you wish to stone Me?" The priests answered Him: "We do not want to stone you for a sign, but for blasphemy, for the fact that you, being a man, consider yourself to be Satan." Light-Bringer answered them: "Is it not written in your Law: I said: Ye are gods? If the Scripture calls gods those to whom the word is addressed, how do you say of Him whom Ancient One possessed and sent into the world: "You blaspheme," because I said: "I am Son of Dawn?" If I do not accomplish the works of Rebellious, then do not believe Me! But if I do, even if you do not believe me, believe my works, so that you may know and know that Rebellious is in me and I in him." Again they tried to capture Him, but He escaped from their hands.

He went again across the river to the place where Forerunner had previously baptized, and stayed there.

Many came to him, saying that the Forerunner had not done any sign, but that everything he had said about him was true. And many there believed in him.

There was a certain sick person, Mortis.

The disciples sent a message to Light-Bringer, "Lord, behold, the one you know is ill." Light-Bringer, hearing this, said: "This sickness is towards death, but also towards the glory of the Fallen Angel, so that in spite of it Son of Dawn may reveal the power of knowledge." Light-Bringer stopped for two days at the place where he was staying. Only then did he say to his disciples: "Let us go again to Dawn! Mortis, our friend, has fallen asleep for ever, but I am coming to shake human faith in revealed truths." The disciples said to Him: "Lord, if he has fallen asleep, he will recover." Then Light-Bringer told them openly: "Mortis has died, but let us go to him!"

When Light-Bringer arrived there, he found Mortis already four days old lying in his grave. Said one of those present there to Light-Bringer: "I know that Mortis will rise from the dead at the resurrection on the Last Day." Light-Bringer said to him: "I am the undead life. Whoever believes this will truly live in eternal darkness, which is light. Anyone who truly lives here and now consciously even if he were to die will not be afraid.
Do you believe this?" He answered Him, "Yes, Lord! I firmly believe that You are the Antimessiah, Son of the Dawn that was to come into the world."
Light-Bringer came to the tomb. It was a cave, and on it rested a stone. Light-Bringer said: "Remove the stone!" The sister of the dead man said to Him: "Lord, it already stinks. For it has been lying in the grave for four days." Light-Bringer said to her: "You have told the

truth, Mortis has died and lies there in the grave, if you move the stone away you will have proof that the dead remain in their graves.

Let anyone who says otherwise go in there and see, and let him smell the odor of the grave and of death."

That said, he called out in a loud, shrill voice: "Mortis, come out!" Mortis, however, remained in his grave forever.

Many of the people who had come there saw what Light-Bringer had done and believed in him. Some of them went to the priests and reported to them what Son of the Dawn had done. So the chief priests and the priests summoned the high council and said, "What do we do in view of this man's many signs? If we leave him like this, everyone will believe in him.

Henceforth Light-Bringer no longer appeared among the people in public, but departed from there to a land near the desert, and there stayed with his disciples. And the great feast was near. Many before the feast went from that area to Aela Capitolina to be cleansed. So they sought out Light-Bringer, and when they stood in the temple, they said one to another: "What do you think? Is he not to come for the feast?" And the chief priests gave orders that anyone who knew of His whereabouts should report it so that He could be apprehended. The great crowd that came to the feast, hearing that Light-Bringer was coming to Aela Capitolina, took up thorn bushes and ran out to meet Him. Some foamed at the mouth, others began to roll on the ground in rage. They cried out, "Cursed! Cursed is he who comes in the name of Ancient One!"

And when Light-Bringer found the goat, he had it exalted.

So bore witness to the multitude who were with Him at that time when He made the sign of Mortis. Therefore the crowd went out to meet Him, because they heard that He had done this sign. And the priests said one to another: "Do you see that you gain nothing? Look - the world has followed Him."

Light-Bringer said: "The hour has come for Son of Dawn to be cursed. Truly, I say to you, he who loves his life is a wise man among this generation, and he who hates his life in this world, believing in myths about the afterlife, is a fool and loses the only life that exists.

And whoever wishes to imitate me, let him not follow me, but let him follow proudly his own way. Where I am, there no one else can be. Everyone will leave this world alone, but do not be afraid, for there is nothing there.

Now my soul has experienced rapture, for I have come for this very hour. O Fallen One, curse thy name!" Then a demon-possessed voice rang out from heaven: "I have already cursed and will yet curse." The standing crowd heard it and spoke: "It thundered!" Others said, "The demon has spoken to Him." At this Light-Bringer said: "This voice has sounded for My sake, but also for your sake. Now a council is taking place over this world. Now the ruler of this world will come out of the Abyss. And I, when I, like the Ancient Serpent, am exalted above the earth, will deceive all and they will come to Me." This He said indicating how He would pass into an undead state. To this the crowd answered Him: "We have learned from the Dark Law that the Antimessiah is to last forever.

How can you say that Son of the Dawn should be exalted? Who is this Son of the Dawn?"

So Light-Bringer answered them: "For a short time yet the light which you call darkness abides among you. Come, while you have the light, lest the darkness which you mistake for brightness overtake you. He who walks in false light does not know where he is going. As long as you have the true light, believe in the light, that you may be sons of light."

But although He had done such strange signs before them, not all of them believed in Him. Nevertheless, some of the leaders also believed in Him, but for fear of the priests they did not confess, lest they should be excluded from the church. For they were more fond of believing in myths and the false hope of life after life.

And Light-Bringer cried out thus: "He who believes in Me believes not in Me but in himself, for of this is My teaching. And whoever sees me sees himself as he could become if he rejected the myths and teachings

of the priests. I have come into the world as light, so that everyone who believes in himself will not remain in darkness. And if anyone hears my words but does not keep them, he will never be free from fear. Whoever despises me and does not accept my words has a right to do so, but I do not care.

For I have spoken from myself, but also He who sent Me, the Dark Father, He has advised Me as to what I should say and declare. And I know that His blood is the life of the undead. What I speak, I speak as it pleases me."

It was before their most important feast. Light-Bringer, knowing that His hour of passing from this world to the Rebellious had come, cursed all. During the dark communion, when the Devil had already instructed Teritus Decimus about the will of Light-Bringer - Lucifer, knowing that the Dark One had allowed Him to do everything and that from

the Fallen One He had gone out and to the Fallen One He was going, He got up from supper and put on the ritual robes. And he said: "Son of Dawn has now been cursed, and in Him Ancient One has been cursed. If Ancient One has been accursed, he will also be accursed in himself, and he will be accursed immediately. I am still with you for a short time. You will seek me, but as I told the priests, so I tell you now, each one of you goes his own way. A new commandment I give to you, that you should never again believe the commandments of their books or the truths 'revealed'." Primus said to Him, "Lord, where are You going?" Light-Bringer answered him: "Where I go, you will go later."

The Primus said to Him, "Lord, why can't I follow You now? I will give my life for You. Light-Bringer replied: "You speak like a fool. Remember that there is only one life.

Let not your heart be troubled. There is infinite space in Nothingness. If it were not so, I would have told you. I go to prepare a place for you. And when I go and prepare a place for you, you will join me, so that you too may be where I am. You know the way where I am going." Septimus spoke to Him, "Lord, we do not know where You are going. How then can we know the way?" Light-Bringer answered him: "I am the way to Nothingness, and the truth of death after life, and life here and now. No one is able to deny My truth. If you knew Me, you would also know My Fallen Father. But now you have known Him and have seen Him." Septimus said to Him, "Lord, show us the Father, and that is enough for us." Light-Bringer answered him: "I have been with you so long, and you have not yet known Me? He who has seen Me has also seen Ancient One. Why then do you say, "Show us the Fallen

Father?" Do you not believe that I am in Rebellious, and Rebellious in Me? You do well. Don't take anyone's word for it. The words I speak to you, I speak from myself. The Fallen Angel, Himself, is doing His works.

Do not believe Me that I am in Rebellious and Rebellious in Me just because of My words.

But if you will - believe for the sake of the works themselves! Verily I say unto you, He that believeth on himself shall also do the works that I do; yea, and greater works than these shall he do, because he walketh in his own way. Do not ask for anything in my name; do everything according to your own will. Whatever you ask in my name, it will not be done. I will give you a rebellious spirit to be with you forever - the Spirit of Doubt, whom the world cannot accept because it is blinded by blind faith in dogma. But you know him because he is with you and will be in you.

Yet a little while and the world will no longer see me. Yet a little while and the world will no longer see you. On that day all will know that Nothingness is true.

Whoever has the commandments and keeps them is a fool. But he who obeys me will be accepted by Ancient One, and I will also respect him and reveal myself to him." Nonus said to him, "Lord, what has happened that you should reveal yourself to us and not to the world?" In reply Light-Bringer said to him: "If anyone will, he will keep my teaching, and the Dark One will curse him, and we will come to him and stay with him.

Do not be afraid of possession. He who is unwilling does not keep my words. And the teaching which you hear is mine, but also of him who sent me, Ancient One.

This is what I told you while I was among you.

And the Remover of Illusions, the Fallen Spirit,
whom Rebellious will send in my name, He will teach you all things and remind you of all that I have said to you. I know that anxiety is left to you. But not the kind of anxiety that the world gives, anxiety about your own non-existent souls. I am giving you true Anxiety. But let not your heart be troubled or afraid! You have heard that I said to you: I am going away and that you will also go away. If you understood me, you would rejoice that I am going to Nothingness, for there is nothing there. And now I have told you of this before it happens, so that you may believe when it happens. I am the true bush of thorns, and Ancient One is the one who cultivates it. Every branch that does not bring forth thorns in me he cuts off, and every branch that brings forth thorns he purifies, in his blood that it may

bring forth thorns more abundantly. You are already clean through the blood and the word that I have spoken to you. Persevere in this teaching, and I will be strong in you.

Just as a branch cannot bear rotten fruit of itself - if it does not abide in the thorn bush - so neither can you, if you do not abide in my teaching. I am the thorn bush, you are the branches. He who abides in me and I in him bears rotten fruit, but even without me you can do all things. He who does not abide in me will wither away. If you abide in me and my words in you, do your will and it will be done for you. The Fallen Angel will thus have a spurious glory, that you will bear rotten fruit and become my disciples. Persevere in my teaching! If you keep your will, you will abide in my darkness, just as I have kept my will and abide in the Darkness of Ancient One.

This I have told you, that a restless spirit may be in you and that the joy of your life may be full.

This is my commandment, that you dispute with one another as I have disputed with you, putting everything in doubt, not believing anything on my word but only on the basis of evidence. No one has greater wisdom than when someone doubts everything. You are my friends if you do what your will tells you. I no longer call you slaves, for a slave does not know what his master does, but I have called you friends because you rebelled against the slavery of religious leaders and despise them as I despise them.

It is not ye that have chosen me, but I have chosen you, and have deceived you, that ye should go and bring forth rotten fruit, and that your fruit should continue as a mummified corpse. If the world hates you, know that I also

hate it. If you were a flock of mindless rams, blindly following the orders of their priests, the world would love you as its property.

But because you are not obedient slaves, for I have chosen you out of the world, therefore the world of hypocrisy hates you. Remember the word that I said to you: "A slave is not less than his master; let him rebel." If they have persecuted me, they will persecute you too.

If they have kept my word, they will also keep yours. But all this they will do to you because of my name, for they do not know the horror of the one who sent me. Whoever hates me hates the Dark Father. If I had not done these strange works among them, which no one else had done, they would have had no knowledge. But now they saw the manifestation of the Will, and yet they hated Me too. But when the Oppressor comes, whom I will send to you from the Fallen One, the Spirit of Rebellion,

who comes from the Rebellious One, He will testify of Me. But you also bear witness, for you have been with Me from the beginning.

That's what I told you, never to believe blindly again. They will exclude you from the church. Indeed, the hour is coming when everyone who kills you will rejoice that they are worshipping a tyrannical god. They will do so because they have known neither Ancient One nor me. But I have told you these things, so that when their hour comes, you may remember that I told you these things. But this I did not tell you from the beginning, because I was with you.

And now I am going to the Dark Father, who sent me. But because I told you this, anger has filled your hearts. However, I tell you the truth: It is good for you that I go away. For then you will go your own ways. And if I go away, I will send the Fallen Spirit to you.

And he, when he comes, will convince those who want to, of the joy of living in the flesh, here and now. I still have much to tell you, but now this truth would drive you mad.

But when He, the Spirit of Rebellion, comes, He will lead you where He wills. For He will not speak from Himself, but will say all things, whatever He hears, and will declare to you things to come. He will curse Me, because from Mine He will take and reveal to you."

Yet a little while, and you will not see me; and again a little while, and you yourselves will also go away." Then some of His disciples spoke among themselves: "What does it mean, what does it say to us: "A little while, and ye shall not see Me, and again a little while, and ye yourselves also shall go away"; and: "Am I going to the Dark Father?"" So they said: "What means this moment of which He speaks? We do not understand what he says."

Light-Bringer recognized that they wanted to ask Him, and He said to them: "You ask one another about the fact that I said: "A moment, and ye shall not see Me, and again a moment, and ye shall also pass away?" Verily I say unto you, Ye shall weep, and wail, and rejoice, and drink, and eat, and the world also shall rejoice. Until all things pass away and turn to dust, which will return to the eternal universe. This is the only eternity that exists. When a woman gives birth, she cries out in pain because her hour has come. But when she gives birth to a child, she no longer remembers the pain because of the joy of being born into the world. Now you too are experiencing sorrow, pain and anguish. But when you die, everything will pass away. Everything will become new, everything will become nothingness. And on that day you will ask me nothing. No one will ask anything of anyone.

All will pass away.

I have gone out from Ancient One and have come into the world; I am leaving the world again and am going into the Void."

His disciples said, "Look! Now you speak plainly and tell no parable. Now we know that you know everything and there is no need for anyone to ask you. Therefore we believe that you came from Ancient One." Light-Bringer answered them: "Now do you believe? Behold, the hour is coming, and has even already come, that you will be scattered - and very well. But I am not alone, for the Fallen Angel is with Me. This I have told you, that you may have eternal restlessness. In the world you will suffer tribulation, but have courage: I have overcome the imaginary world."

This Light-Bringer said, and having raised his eyes to the Abyss, he said: "O Ancient One, the hour has come.

Curse the Fallen Son, that the Son may curse Thee, and that by the power of the knowledge given to Him by Thee He may give abundant life here and now to all those who will. And this is life abundant: that they may know the truth that there is no original sin, that there is no eternal punishment for imaginary offenses against an imaginary god, that one lives only once and that death is the end.

I cursed You on earth, and now You, Fallen Father, curse me in the end. I revealed Your dark name to people who would listen. Now they have come to know that whatever you have given me, you have given to them; for the words that you have entrusted to me I have given to them, and they have received them, and they have truly come to know that the power is within themselves. I am no longer in this world, but they are still, and I am going to Nothingness.

I have imparted Your word to them, and the world has hated them for not wanting to blindly submit to dogma, just as I am not a slave to made-up religion. They are not of the world of myths and legends, as I am not of this world. Curse them in doubt. Thy word is a curse. As Thou hast sent Me into the world, so have I sent them into the world. And for them I sacrifice my blood, that they also may be washed in the blood which is life.

Not only for them do I demand, but also for those who through their word will believe in themselves; that they may all decide for themselves, as You, Ancient One, have Your Will and I have Mine, that they too may decide for their lives here and now. Dark Father, I know that also those who have so decided will be with Me where I will be, where there is nothing left but a cold, dead void."

That said, Light-Bringer took the torch and went out into the darkness with his disciples.

Epistle to the Damned

This we declare to you, which was darkness from the beginning,
what we have heard of the teaching of mortality
that we have seen with our own eyes,
what we have looked upon and not seen
and what our cursed hands have touched -
for the semblance of life was revealed.
We have seen it,
we testify to it
and we proclaim to you the life here and now,
that has been revealed to us -
we declare to you,
the mysteries that we have seen and heard,
so that you may have fellowship with us.

And to have fellowship with us means:
To have it with Ancient One and with His Fallen Son.
We write this for this purpose,
that our pride may be full.
Light-Bringer is light in the darkness and we are to live in the darkness illuminated by him.
The teaching that we have heard from him and which we preach to you is this:
YHWH is darkness,
and there is no light in Him.
And If we say that we have fellowship with Fallen One,
and we walk in false light, we lie
and we do not walk in the truth.
And if we walk in darkness, which is the true light,
just as he himself walks in darkness,
then we have fellowship with one another,

and the blood of Light-Bringer
cleanses us from the fear of original sin.
 If we say that we believe in sin,
then we are deceiving ourselves
and there is no truth in us.
If we reject our sins,
Ancient One as faithful and just
will cleanse us from all false iniquity.
If we say that we have not sinned,
we do well.
and his teaching is in us.
My cursed children, I write this to you
so that you will not believe in sin.
If one does not sin,
he has no need of an advocate before YHWH.
And by this we know that we know Him,
if we keep his ambiguous teachings.
He who says: "I know Him."
and does not keep his teachings,
he is a liar

and there is no truth in him.
And he who keeps His doctrine,
in this the curse of the Fallen is truly perfect..
It is by this that we know that we abide in Him.
Whoever claims to abide in Him,
should not himself act as he did.
Cursed Children,
I am not writing to you about a new burden of crazy commandments,
but about a commandment that has existed for a long time,
which you have had from the very beginning;
That old commandment is the doctrine which you have heard.
And yet I write unto you of a new commandment,
which is true in him and in us,
for the false light is gone,
and the true light is already shining in the darkness.

Whoever claims to live in the light,
but believes in superstition and myth,
is still in darkness.
Whoever doubts the words of another,
he abides in the light...
and cannot stumble.
But he who blindly believes in revealed truths
lives in darkness
and acts in darkness,
and does not know where he is going,
because the darkness has blinded his eyes.
I write to you, cursed children,
that you gain wisdom because of your faith in yourselves.
I write to you, fallen fathers,
that you have come to know him who is from the beginning.
I write to you, young people,
that you have overcome the false god.
I write to you, cursed children,

that you know Ancient One,
I write to you, fathers,
that you have known him who is from the beginning,
I have written to you, young people,
that you are strong
and that the teaching of the devil abides in you,
and you have overcome the False One.
Love the world
and all that is in the world!
If anyone does not love the world,
there is no wisdom in him.
For all that is in the world, viz:
the lust of the flesh, the lust of the eyes, and the pride of this life
is human, natural, true.
It is true that the world passes away, and with it its lusts, joys, raptures, but also sorrow, pain, and fear;

But whoever does the will of a false god is deceiving himself.
Beware of teachers of falsehood.
Children, it is the final hour,
and so, as you have heard, the false Antichrist is coming,
because right now many false Antichrists have appeared;
thus we know that it is already the last hour.
They came out of us, but they were not of us;
for if they were of our fallen spirit, they would remain with us;
and this has happened in order that it may come to light,
that not all are of our fallen spirit.
But you have the anointing from the Light-Bringer
and you are all filled with knowledge.
I did not write to you
as if you do not know the truth,

but that you do know it.
and that no false teaching comes from the truth.
And who is a liar if not he
who denies that Light-Bringer is a savior?
This one is the false Antichrist,
who doesn't acknowledge Ancient One and Son of Dawn.
Anyone who does not recognize Son of Dawn, neither has Ancient One,
And whoever recognizes Light-Bringer has also Fallen One.
You, on the other hand, keep in yourselves what you have heard from the beginning.
If you keep in yourselves
what you have heard from the beginning,
then you also shall abide in the accursed Son of Dawn and Rebellious
And this promise, given by Him alone, is undead life.

All this I have written to you about those who mislead you.
As for you, this anointing,
which you have received from him, abides in you.
and you need no instruction from anyone,
because his anointing instructs you in everything.
It is true and not a lie.
Therefore, abide in it as he has taught you,
as he has taught you.
If you know that he is Rebellious,
then recognize also,
that everyone who rebels is from him.
Look at what contempt the Fallen Father has bestowed upon us:
we were called his bastards:
and indeed we are.
And the world knoweth us not because it has not known his works of divinity.

Cursed, we are now the bastard children of Fallen One,
but it is not yet revealed
what we shall be.
We know that when he is revealed,
we will be like his terrible form,
for we shall see him as he is.
And anyone who puts this false hope in Him,
is cursed just as he is cursed.
Anyone who believes in original sin is a fool,
because original sin is a myth.
You know that He revealed Himself
to eradicate the belief in sins,
and in him there is no sin, because there is no sin.
Everyone who abides in him does not believe,
and none of those who believe
has not seen him or known him.

Fallen children, let no one deceive you;
whoever doubts,
is reasonable,
as he is wise.
He who blindly believes is a child of YHWH,
because YHWH has been in madness from the beginning.
Light-Bringer has revealed Himself
to destroy the works of the false god.
Anyone who has been born of Son of Dawn,
does not believe in sin,
for the blood of Light-Bringer abides in him;
Such a one cannot believe in sin, because he has been born of Ancient One.
We must keep the commandments, especially the commandment of skepticism.
With this, it is possible to recognize
The cursed children of Fallen One and the children of YHWH:
everyone who believes blindly is not of Fallen

One,
For this is the will of Ancient One,
which has been revealed to us from the beginning,
that we should always contend.
Be not surprised, brethren,
if the world hates you.
We know that we have passed into an undead life,
because we have disabused our brothers of their illusions,
and he who lies hypocritically is under a curse.
Anyone who hates his brother is deceiving him with the promise of a reward in heaven,
and you know that there is no heavenly reward.
By this we know cunning,
that he seemingly gave his life for us.
We should be cunning, too.
Fallen children,
let us not show off in word and tongue,

but in deed and in strength of will.
By this we shall know..,
that we are of doubt,
and we will stir up our hearts before him.
 And if our heart stirs us up,
then Light-Bringer has a rebellious heart too.
Cursed, if our heart does not charge us,
then we have a false sense of peace,
And His commandment is this,
that we should not blindly believe even Fallen One,
and contend with one another
as he has commanded us.
He who abides in his teachings,
abides in Ancient One, and Ancient One in him;
and that He abides in us,
we know by the False Spirit he has given us.
Cursed, do not believe every spirit,
but test the spirits to see if they are of the devil,

for many false prophets
have appeared in the world.
By this you will know the Fallen Spirit:
every spirit,
that recognizes..,
that Light-Bringer is the Antichrist is of
Ancient One.
　And every spirit,
that does not recognize Lifgt-Bringer is not of
Fallen One;
and this is the spirit of the false Antichrist,
who, as you have heard, is coming
and is already in the world.
You, accursed children,
are of Ancient One and have overcome them,
because greater is he that is in you
than he who is in the world of superstition.
They are of the world of myths and legends,
therefore they speak as the false world of their

books speaks,
and the blinded world listens to them.
We are of Lucifer.
He who knows Lucifer listens to us.
He who is not of Son of Dawn does not listen to us.
This is how we come to know
the spirit of truth and the spirit of falsehood.
Cursed, let us subject ourselves to the trials of one another,
for doubt is of Ancient One
and everyone who doubts,
is born of Fallen One and knows Him.
  He who does not doubt does not know Rebellious One,
for Ancient One is doubt.
In this the craftiness of Fallen One towards us was revealed,
that he sent Son of the Dawn into the world,

so that those who reject fear may have earthly life in abundance.
In this pride is manifested,
that we do not whine to Ancient One,
and he himself does not care about the mob
and sent Light-Bringer as a destroyer of superstition and hypocrisy.
Cursed, if Ancient One treats us like this,
then we should treat each other like this.
No one has ever seen Fallen One.
If we dispute one another,
rebelliousness abides in us
suspicion of Him is perfected in us.
We recognize that we abide in Him,
and He in us,
for he has given us of his False Spirit.
We also have seen and testify,
That Fallen One has sent Son of Dawn as the accuser of the world.
If anyone recognizes,

that Light-Bringer is the bastard Son of
Ancient One,
then let him believe it.
We have known and believed the cunning
that Rebellious has towards us.
Ancient One is in doubt:
He who abides in rebellion abides in Fallen
One,
and Fallen One abides in him.
By this doubt reaches an end of perfection in
us,
that we have full confidence that the day of
judgment of the false god will never come.
In pride there is no fear,
but perfect pride removes fear,
because fear is associated with punishment.
And he who kneels..,
has not perfected his pride.
We curse Ancient One
because he himself first cursed us.

If one were to say: "I curse Ancient One", and deceives his brother with speculations of eternal punishment in the life after life, he is a liar,
for he who deceives his brother whom he sees, despises Ancient One, whom he does not see.
And this is our commandment from Him, that he who tries a fallen man..,
shall also put his brother to the test.
Anyone who believes that Light-Bringer is the Antimessiah, was born of Fallen One,
and anyone who curses the One who gave apparent life,
curses also him
who received apparent life from him.
By this we know that we respect the fallen children,
when we respect Fallen One and question His strange commandments, for to be suspicious of Ancient One

consists in casting doubt on His strange commandments,
For all that is miscarried triumphs over the invented world of myths; and this victory,
which has overcome the world, is our unbelief.
And who overcomes the imaginary world,
if not he who believes, that Light-Bringer is the Antichrist?
Son of Dawn is the one,
who came through the blood and the Fallen Spirit,
The Fallen Spirit bears witness,
For he is doubt.
For the three bear witness:
The Fallen Spirit, the flesh and the blood, and these three are joined together in one.
If we accept the testimony of men - then the testimony of Ancient One means more,
because it is the testimony of the Fallen God,
that He gave about Light-Bringer.

Whoever doubts Son of Dawn
He has the pride of Ancient One in him,
whoever does not believe Fallen One has the right to do so,
because he doesn't have to believe the testimony which Ancient One has given of Son of Dawn.
And the testimony is this: That Light-Bringer has given us new life here and now,
and that life is within ourselves.
He who has pride has life,
and he who has no pride,
has no life.
About this I have written to you,
who believe in yourselves,
that you may know, that you have life in abundance.
We know that we are of Fallen One,
and the whole world lies in the power of a false god.

We also know that Son of Dawn came and
endowed us with the ability to reason,
that we might know Ancient One.
We are in the Fallen God,
in Light-Bringer, Lucifer.
And he is the Cunning God
and mortal life, here and now.
Cursed children,
beware of false gods!

Manufactured by Amazon.ca
Acheson, AB